CHRISTMAS JOKES

'Mum, how long is it until Christmas?'

'It's still a few months away, darling. Why do you ask?'

'I was wondering if I had to start being good yet.'

First published 2017 by Macmillan Children's Books
an imprint of Pan Macmillan
20 New Wharf Road, London N1 9RR
Associated companies throughout the world
www.panmacmillan.com

ISBN 978-1-5098-6035-7

3 5 7 9 8 6 4

A CIP catalogue record for this book is available from
the British Library.

Compiled and illustrated by Dan Newman
Printed and bound by CPI Group (UK) Ltd, Croydon CR0 4YY

CHRISTMAS JOKES

MACMILLAN CHILDREN'S BOOKS

What did one angel
say to the other angel?
'Halo there.'

What's green, hangs in a
doorway and croaks?
A mistle-toad.

I told Grandad that a
lot of people go to
Amazon to choose
Christmas presents.

Three days later, he rang
me from Brazil.

What's different
about the alphabet at
Christmas?

It has no 'L'.

What's the Internet's
favourite carol?

'Oh .com All Ye Faithful'.

What squeaks
and is scary?

The Ghost of
Christmouse past.

Our local bookshop
had a Christmas
sale with a third off
everything.

I bought a copy of
The Lion, the Witch.

'Why was that security
guard talking to you?'

'He told me off for trying
to do my Christmas
shopping early.'

'Why is that a problem?'

'Well, the shop wasn't
actually open.'

We like to cut down our own Christmas tree.

We call it Christmas chopping.

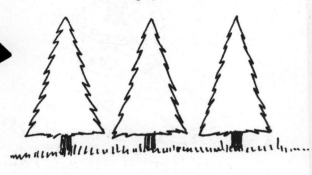

What do hedgehogs eat for lunch?

Prickled onions.

What do crackers,
fruitcake and nuts
remind me of?

You!

'Doctor, I'm so excited
about Christmas that
I can't get to sleep.'

'Well, try lying right on
the very edge of your bed.
You'll soon drop off.'

Why do birds fly
south in the winter?

**Because it's too
far to walk!**

'Doctor, I'm afraid I've got a
mince pie stuck in my ear.'

**'Well, I can put some
cream on it.'**

What is a parent's
favourite Christmas carol?

'Silent Night'.

What do elves write in
Christmas cards?

**Wishing you a
fairy Merry
Christmas!**

Why do mummies like
Christmas presents?

Because of the wrapping.

What did the salt say to the pepper on Christmas morning?

'Seasoning's Greetings.'

How do snowmen greet each other?

It's ice to meet you.

What did the Christmas card say to the stamp?

'Stick with me and we'll go places.'

What's the difference
between Saint George
and one of Father
Christmas's reindeer?

One slays a dragon, the
other's draggin' a sleigh.

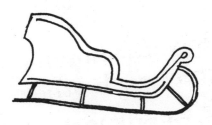

What sort of ball
doesn't bounce?

A snowball.

What did the bag of salt & vinegar say to the bag of cheese & onion?

'Merry Crisp-mas.'

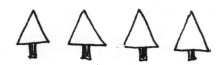

Where will you find a Christmas tree?

Between Christmas two and Christmas four.

What Christmas carol gets sung in the desert?

'O Camel Ye Faithful'.

Why can't Christmas
trees knit?

Because they drop
their needles.

How does Good King
Wenceslas like his pizza?

Deep pan, crisp and even.

What comes at
the end of
Christmas Day?
The letter Y.

Where do ghosts go for a
treat at Christmas?

The phantomime.

What does December have
that other months don't?

The letter D.

What's the loudest part
of a Christmas tree?

The bark.

What's the difference
between a postbox and
a polar bear's bum?

**If you don't know,
I think I'll post my own
Christmas cards.**

Perfect Presents

What's the first thing you should give your parents at Christmas?

A list of everything you want.

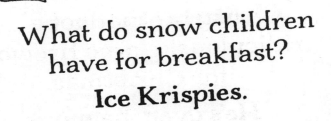

What do snow children have for breakfast?

Ice Krispies.

What present should you
give a tiny ballerina who's
too small for a tutu?

A one-one.

What's the best
Christmas present?

**A broken drum – you
can't beat it.**

My brother got a
ridiculously large firework
for Christmas.

He's over the moon.

I wasn't happy getting a pocket calculator for Christmas.

I already know how to count my pockets.

What do you give a hip-hop singer for Christmas?

It doesn't matter, as long as you wrap it.

What present do you give a brass band who've broken all their instruments?

A tuba glue.

Dad got a pair of trousers made from spider silk.

They look great, but the flies keep sticking.

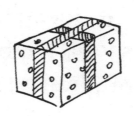

What did the farmer get for Christmas?

A cow-culator.

What's the perfect musical gift for a Spanish fisherman?

Cast-a-nets.

'I got a giant pack of playing cards for Christmas!'

'Big deal.'

Dad got a box set
of *Doctor Who* for
Christmas.
We watched it
back to back.

**Unfortunately
I wasn't the one
facing the telly.**

I think Father Christmas
is on a budget this year.

**Mum asked for something
with diamonds in it . . .
she got a pack of cards.**

'Excuse me, I'd like to get a kitten for my son.'

'Sorry, we don't do swaps.'

'No, I mean do you have any kittens going cheap?'

'Of course not, they all go miaow.'

Man: 'That train set looks brilliant, I'll take it.'

Assistant: 'Good choice, sir. I'm sure your son will love it.'

Man: 'Oh yes . . . I suppose he will. You'd better give me two then.'

'My Christmas stocking
has a hole in it!'

'Of course it does.
How else can Father
Christmas put the
presents in?'

For Christmas I wished
to have my name up in
lights all over the world.

So Mum and Dad
changed my name
to 'EXIT'.

What do witches
use to wrap
their presents?
Spell-otape.

I bought my
son a fridge for
Christmas.

**I can't wait to see
his face light up
when he opens it.**

Christmas Books

The Art of Kissing
    by Miss L. Toe

Winning at Charades
    by Vic Tree

Guessing your Presents
    by P. King

Bad Gifts
    by M. T. Box

How to get a Great Present
    by B. Good

Last Christmas I got a really cheap dictionary from my sister.

I couldn't find the words *to thank her.*

What do you give a dog for Christmas?

A mobile bone.

I wanted to get my dad some camouflage trousers for Christmas.

I couldn't find any.

I can't decide what to give my little brother for Christmas this year . . .

Last year I gave him chickenpox.

I dreamed Father Christmas gave me a giant marshmallow as a present.

When I woke up my pillow was missing.

For Christmas I got
a book about how they
fix ships together.

It's riveting.

'Do you have any of
those pink toy cars?'

**'We've sold out, I'm afraid.
Absolutely everyone in the
whole country has bought
one this week.'**

'What do you mean?'

**'We've turned into a
pink car-nation.'**

'Dad, can I have
a wombat for
Christmas?'

'A wombat?
What do you want
a wombat for?'

'To play wom.'

Father Christmas gave
me a huge ball of clay
this year.

I don't know what
to make of it.

Why do mummies like
Christmas so much?

**Because of all
the wrapping.**

I was going to give Dad
a broken pencil, but I
changed my mind.

There was no point.

I think we're going to the
cinema at Christmas to
see a film about caravans.

I've seen the trailer.

'What would you like
for Christmas? I was
thinking of getting you
a PlayStation.'

'Nothing would make
me happier!'

'OK, I'll get you
nothing then.'

We wanted some
fireworks at Christmas,
but Dad didn't light them
at the right time.

He was bang out
of order.

Father Christmas

Christmas Books

*What Do You
Do After Christmas
Dinner?*
by Clare Inup

Sledging for Beginners
by I. C. Bottom

Surprise Present!
by Omar Gosh

Father Christmas
is so strong, he can
lift a reindeer with
one hand.

The problem is, he
can't find a one-
handed reindeer
to prove it.

What's as big as
Father Christmas but
weighs nothing?

His shadow.

What did Father
Christmas call the
reindeer with two short
legs and two long legs?
Eileen.

What did he call the
reindeer with one eye
higher than the other?
Isaiah.

What did he call the
reindeer with three humps
on its back?
Humphrey.

Who delivers
Christmas presents
to pets?

Santa Paws.

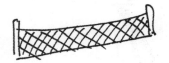

What did Father
Christmas call the
reindeer that was lying
across his tennis court?

Annette.

And what did he call
the reindeer who was
standing across a river?

Bridget.

What is a skunk's
favourite Christmas
song?

'Jingle Smells'.

What did Father
Christmas's scarf say
to his hat?

'You go on ahead,
I'll hang around here.'

Is Father Christmas
an employee?
No, he's elf-employed.

What did the spider
want for Christmas?
A new web-site.

What did Father Christmas
say to Mrs Christmas when
he looked out of the window?
'Looks like rain, dear.'

What makes Father
Christmas such a
good racing driver?

**He's always in
Pole position.**

Father Christmas was
inspecting the reindeer
with his wife.

**'This one's legs look
a little short,' he said.**

**'How long do you want
them?' she replied. 'They
reach all the way to the
ground, don't they?'**

How does Father
Christmas get four
reindeer in his sleigh?

Two on the front bench,
and two on the back.

And how does he get four
polar bears in his sleigh?

He takes the reindeer out.

Who is Father Christmas's
favourite singer?

Elf-is Presley.

What photos does
Father Christmas take?

Elfies.

And what does he use
to take them?

His North Polaroid.

Father Christmas lost his enormous giant reindeer, and his tiny baby reindeer.

He looked high and low for them.

How many presents can Father Christmas fit in an empty sleigh?

Just one. After that, it isn't empty.

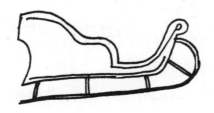

Where does Father
Christmas go swimming?
The North Pool.

What does Father
Christmas say when he
sees a herd of reindeer in
the distance?

**'Look, a herd of reindeer
in the distance.'**

What does he say when
he sees a herd of reindeer
with sunglasses on?

**Nothing. He doesn't
recognize them.**

What does he say when he sees a group of polar bears in sunglasses?

'Aha! You fooled me once with those disquises, but not this time!'

How can you tell when Father Christmas is in your house?

You can sense his presents.

Why doesn't Father Christmas go down some chimneys?

Elf and Safety regulations.

What goes 'Oh, oh, oh'?

Father Christmas walking backwards.

What can Father Christmas give to everyone and still keep?

A cold.

Why does
Father Christmas climb
down chimneys?

Because it soots him.

How can Father
Christmas tell if there's a
reindeer in his fridge?

He looks for hoof prints
in the butter.

If he's feeling lazy, Father Christmas feeds the reindeer in his pyjamas.

How they get in his pyjamas is a mystery.

What do you call Father Christmas when he's lying on the beach?

Sandy Claus.

What do you get if
you cross Father
Christmas with a duck?
A Christmas quacker.

What do you call
Father Christmas
when he doesn't move?
Santa Pause.

Why does Father
Christmas buy treats for
his elf mathematicians?
**Because it's the little things
that count.**

What's red and white
and red and white
and red and white?

**Father Christmas
rolling down a hill.**

Father Christmas
wasn't too sure about
his beard at first.

**Then it grew
on him.**

Father Christmas
experimented with battery-
powered robot reindeer, but
they weren't any good.

**They didn't charge
quickly enough.**

What's red and white
and goes up and down,
up and down,
up and down?

**Father Christmas
on a bungee rope.**

What happened when
Father Christmas fell
asleep in a fireplace?

He slept like a log.

Father Christmas
had a couple of spare
reindeer, so he decided
to sell them on eBay
for £500.

Nobody put in a bid,
because they were
two deer.

Why is it so cold at
Christmas?

Because it's Decembrrrrr.

Why does Father
Christmas cry on
26 December?

He gets Santa-mental.

Why didn't Father
Christmas get wet when
he lost his umbrella?

It wasn't raining.

On which side of
Father Christmas's
face is his beard?

The outside.

Why does Father
Christmas worry about
getting stuck
up a chimney?

He's Claus-trophobic.

What kind of motorbike
does Father Christmas
ride?

A Holly-Davidson.

What is Father
Christmas's wife called?

Mary Christmas.

How do you show your
appreciation for Father
Christmas?

Sant-applause.

Why does Father Christmas have three gardens?

So that he can hoe, hoe, hoe.

Father Christmas was just about throw away all his socks . . .

Then he got cold feet.

What kind of coat does Father Christmas wear if it rains on Christmas Eve?

A wet one.

What do you call
a smelly Santa?

Farter Christmas.

What did Father
Christmas do when a
reindeer ate his pen?

He used a pencil.

Life at the North Pole

How do you get milk
from a polar bear?

Wait until it's asleep,
open its fridge very
quietly, grab the milk,
then run like mad.

Why do reindeer
wear bells?

Because their horns
don't work.

How do you speak to a large, angry polar bear?

From a great distance.

Why do reindeer have fur coats?

Because they'd look silly in woolly jumpers.

What's the difference
between a reindeer
and a teabag?

If you don't know
I'm not going to ask you
to make me tea.

Which reindeer has
the worst manners?

Rude-olph.

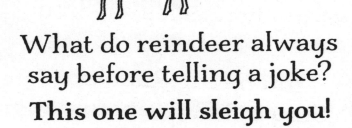

What do reindeer always
say before telling a joke?

This one will sleigh you!

What's furry, round
and smells minty?
A Polo bear.

'Keep that reindeer out
of my house! It's covered
in fleas!'

**'You heard, Rudolph.
Stay out of the house –
it's covered in fleas.'**

What time is it
when a polar bear
sits on your igloo?

Time to get a new igloo.

What often falls at the
North Pole but never
gets hurt?

Snow.

Why do seals swim
in salt water?

**Because pepper water
makes them sneeze.**

How do you tell the difference between a walrus and an orange?

Try giving one a squeeze. If you don't get orange juice, it's the walrus.

What's the difference between a polar bear and a banana?

You'd better find out, because if you try to peel a polar bear . . .

Why shouldn't you take a reindeer to the zoo?

Because they prefer the movies.

What has eight legs, four antlers and two noses?

Two reindeer!

How did Rudolph learn to read?

He was elf-taught.

How many of Father
Christmas's reindeer
can jump higher
than a pine tree?

**All of them – pine trees
can't jump.**

What do you call a
reindeer wearing earmuffs?

**Anything you like.
He can't hear you.**

What do reindeer use to decorate their antlers?

Horn-aments.

How does Rudolph know when Christmas is coming?

He checks his calen-deer.

25

What's the difference between a cookie and a reindeer?

Try dunking them in your milk – then you'll know.

Why was the reindeer
wearing black boots?
**All his brown ones
were muddy.**

Where would Rudolph
go if he lost his tail?
To a re-tail shop.

What do you call
a reindeer with
no eyes?

No idea.

What do you call a
reindeer with no eyes
and no legs?

Still no idea.

What do reindeer have
that no other animals do?

Baby reindeer.

Why was Rudolph
such a bad dancer?

**Because he had
two left feet.**

Polar bears are three metres
tall and weigh 400kg.
Where do they sleep?

Anywhere they like.

Why did the reindeer
say 'woof'?

He was learning a
foreign language.

What do snowmen
eat for breakfast?

Snowflakes.

How do you stop a
reindeer from smelling?

Put your fingers
up its nose.

Why don't reindeer
ride motorbikes?
Their antlers won't
fit in a helmet.

What's white, lives at
the North Pole and runs
around naked?

A polar bare.

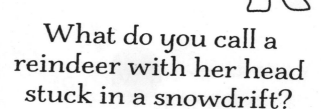

What do you call a
reindeer with her head
stuck in a snowdrift?

Anything you like.
She can't hear you.

A seal will dive down
hundreds of metres
for fish ...

Imagine what he'd do
for a portion of chips!

What do you call a
skeleton at the North Pole?

A numbskull.

What's wrong with a
reindeer with jelly in one ear
and custard in the other?

He's a trifle deaf.

What's the difference
between a blueberry
and a polar bear?

They're both blue, except
for the polar bear.

What says 'Now you see
me, now you don't, now you
see me, now you don't'?

A snowman on a
zebra crossing.

Santa's Little Helpers

Where do you
usually find elves?

Depends where
you left them.

Who holds all
Father Christmas's
books for him?

The books-elf.

What do elves pay
for the bells on
their hats?

Jingle bills.

What do elves make their
sandwiches from?

Shortbread.

What do Santa's
elves have for tea?

Fairy cakes.

Who is always
following the first
eleven elves?

The tw-elf.

Who runs the
North Pole Hospital?

The National Elf Service.

What did the elves
do when a polar
bear ran off with
their football?

They played tennis.

Who is the smelliest elf?
Stinkerbell.

One of the elves is so
short that when he pulls
up his socks he can't see
where he's going.

How many elves
does it take to change
a light bulb?

Ten. One to change
the bulb and nine
underneath him,
standing on each
other's shoulders.

What do elves
learn at school?

The elf-abet.

What do you call
an elf who has just
won the lottery?

Welfy.

How long is an elf's shoe?
One foot long.

What do elves play
on their days off?

Miniature golf.

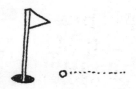

What cars do elves drive?

**Either a Mini . . .
or a Toy-ota.**

Why did Father Christmas tell off one of his elves at dinner?

Because he was a-gobblin'.

When are the elves going to arrive?
Shortly.

Why did the elf go to
bed with a ruler?

He wanted to see if
he slept longer.

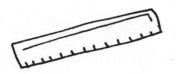

What time do the elves
start work?

Shortly after nine.

Why did the elf's
photos look rubbish?

**They were all
pixie-lated.**

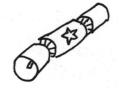

What do elves have
for lunch?

**An hour, like
everyone else.**

Chilly Chuckles

What's an ig?

A snow house with no loo.

What do snowmen and
snow-women have?

Chill-dren.

What do you call
a snowman in
summer?

A puddle.

How do I build a
shelter in the snow?

I-gloo it together.

What happened to
the snowman with
the fiery temper?

He had a meltdown.

Where do
snowmen
dance?

Snow balls.

How do you scare a
snowman?

Plug in a hairdryer.

What do you sing at a
snowman's birthday
party?

'Freeze a jolly
good fellow'.

How do snowmen
get around?

By icicle.

Where do snowmen
keep their money?

In a snow bank.

And what do they call
their money?

Iced lolly.

What do snowmen
eat for lunch?

Ice-bergers.

And what do they put
on them?

Chilly sauce.

What do snowmen
do at weekends?

Just chill out.

Why did the
snowman stand on
the marshmallow?

Because he didn't
want to fall in the
hot chocolate.

What did the snowflake
say to the snowman?

Nothing. Snowflakes
can't talk.

What does a bald
snowman need?

An ice cap.

How can you tell
a snowman is angry
with you?

He gives you the
cold shoulder.

What's white and floats upwards?

A lost snowflake.

What did the snow-policeman say to the snow-burglar?

'Freeze!'

What did one
snowman say to the
other snowman?
'Can you smell
carrots?'

What do Mexican
snowmen eat?
Brrr-itos . . . with
lots of chilly beans.

Eating and Drinking

What's the difference
between bogeys and
Brussels sprouts?

Kids will eat bogeys.

What's the key to a great
Christmas dinner?

A tur-key.

What two things should you never eat before breakfast on Christmas Day?
Lunch and dinner.

'Mum, I think this Christmas pudding is off.'
'Off? Where to?'

There are two
kinds of people at
Christmas.

People who eat too
much chocolate,
and liars.

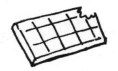

Who's never hungry
at Christmas?

The turkey, because
it's always stuffed.

What do you get if you cross a turkey with an octopus?

Enough drumsticks for everybody.

Last year's turkey really tickled the palate.

Mum forgot to take the feathers off.

What do you call someone who's eaten a whole Christmas turkey?

An ambulance.

Mum: 'You've been no help this Christmas.'

Dad: 'What do you mean? I bought the turkey, and plucked it, and stuffed it. Now all you've got to do is kill it and put it in the oven.'

Last Christmas Mum's gravy was very thick. When she stirred it, the room went round.

'I'm worried that the Christmas cake I gave you was a bit hard.'

'Oh, don't worry – it was perfect.'

'Really?'

'Yes, a slice was just right to fix our wobbly table.'

Who beats his chest,
swings from
Christmas cake to
Christmas cake and
smells of almonds?

Tarzipan.

Why did the Christmas
cake go to the doctor?

Because he felt crummy.

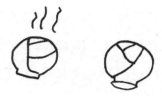

Mum: 'Eat your Brussels sprouts – they're good for growing children.'

Son: 'Why would I want to grow children?'

What do zombies put on their Christmas dinner?

Grave-y.

How do you tell the
difference between
tinned turkey and
tinned ham?

Read the labels.

Who hides in a bakery
at Christmas?

A mince spy.

Why is a Christmas cake
like the sea?

**Because it's full of
currants.**

What do
redcurrants say
to each other at
Christmas?

"Tis the season
to be jelly!'

How do you find out
if a turkey is stupid
and foolish?

Ask if it's looking
forward to
Christmas.

Festive Animals

What do you call a chicken
at the North Pole?

Lost.

Who brings presents to all
the little furry creatures?
Father Christmouse.

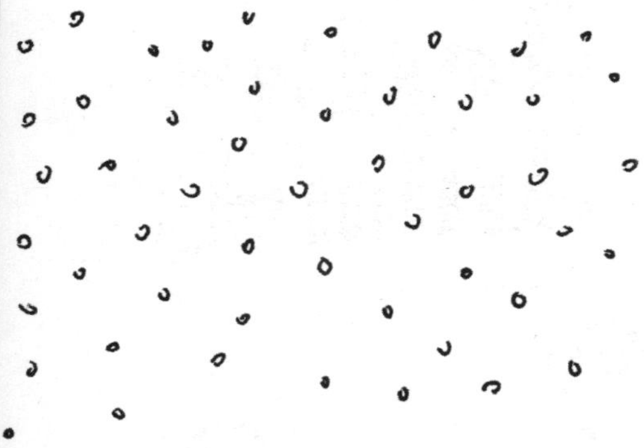

What sort of
insects love snow?

Mo-ski-toes.

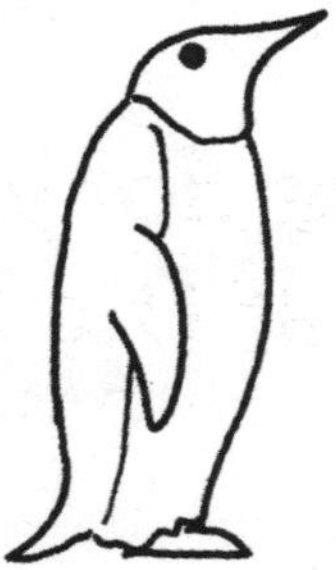

Which bird
should you ask
to write your
Christmas cards?

**A ballpoint
pen-quin.**

Who brings presents to all the little sharks?

Santa Jaws.

Why did the turkey join a band?

Because it already had the drumsticks.

What do you get if you cross a snowman with a shark?

Frostbite.

What do sheep say
to each other on
Christmas morning?

'**Merry Christmas to
ewe . . . and season's
bleatings.**'

What do angry rodents
send each other in
December?

Cross-mouse cards.

Why wouldn't the baby lobster share her Christmas presents?

Because she's a little shellfish.

How do you get four walruses in a Mini?

Two in the front, two in the back.

How do you get four Father Christmases in a Mini?

Don't be silly, there's only one Father Christmas.

How do you know there
are two walruses in
your fridge?

You hear giggling when
the light goes out.

How do you know there
are three walruses in
your fridge?

You can't close the door.

How do you know there
are four walruses in
your fridge?

There's an empty Mini
parked outside.

What's a dog's
favourite carol?

'Bark! The Herald
Angels Sing'.

Why don't polar bears
eat penguins?

They can't get the
wrappers off.

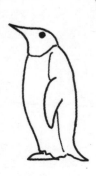

What do you get if you cross Father Christmas with a duck?

A Christmas quacker.

What do you call polar bears with no ears?

Polar b.

Knock Knock!

Knock knock!
Who's there?
Gladys.
Gladys who?
Gladys nearly Christmas!

Knock knock!
Who's there?
Hannah.
Hannah who?
Hannah partridge in a
pear tree.

Knock knock!
Who's there?
Arthur.
Arthur who?
Arthur any more
mince pies?

Knock knock!
Who's there?
Our Wayne.
Our Wayne who?
Our Wayne in a manger,
no crib for a bed . . .

Knock knock!
Who's there?
Holly.
Holly who?
Holly-days are
here again.

Knock knock!
Who's there?
Doughnut.
Doughnut who?
Doughnut open until
Christmas!

Knock knock!
Who's there?
Police.
Police who?
Police don't make
me eat Brussels
sprouts again.

Knock knock!
Who's there?
Mary and Abby.
Mary and Abby who?
Mary Christmas and
Abby New Year!

Knock knock!
Who's there?
Wanda!
Wanda who?
Wanda know what you're getting for Christmas?

Knock knock!
Who's there?
Rabbit.
Rabbit who?
Rabbit carefully – it's a Christmas present.

Knock knock!
Who's there?
Irish.
Irish who?
Irish you a Merry
Christmas!

Knock knock!
Who's there?
Snow.
Snow who?
Snow use – I've
forgotten my name again!

Knock knock!
Who's there?
Wenceslas.
Wenceslas who?
Wenceslas train home?

Knock knock!
Who's there?
Oakham.
Oakham who?
Oakham all ye faithful ...

Knock knock!
Who's there?
Avery.
Avery who?
Avery Merry Christmas!

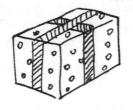

Knock knock!
Who's there?
Elf.
Elf who?
**Elf me wrap this
present for Santa!**

One Christmas,
It Was So Cold...

... we would empty the freezer and huddle round it to get warm.

... words would freeze as you spoke them. You had to grab them out of the air and thaw them out by the fire to find out what someone had said!

... dogs would be stuck
to lamp posts.

... I needed a hammer
and chisel to get my
coat off.

... when farmers
milked their cows,
they got ice cream.

One Christmas, it was so cold . . .

. . . I chipped a tooth on my soup.

. . . when I tried to open my post, the letter snapped.

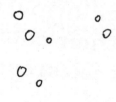

... when I turned on the shower, it hailed.

... my shadow stuck to the ground. When I walked off, it shattered.

... Dad started using chilli sauce as aftershave so that he could feel his face.

One Christmas, it was so cold . . .

. . . the fog froze and I had to dig a tunnel to school.

. . . I had to break the smoke off my chimney.

. . . when Dad tried to take the rubbish out, it refused to go.

. . . wee-cicles. (You know what I'm talking about.)

Christmas Stories

A collection of festive tales

Festive tales of snow,
sparkles, family,
friends, presents and
princesses from some of the
nation's favourite storytellers

Includes stories from:

Julia Donaldson, Malorie
Blackman, Philip Ardagh,
Adèle Geras, Richmal Crompton,
Robert Westall, Anna Wilson,
Karen McCombie, Rumer Godden,
Martin Waddell and Shirley Climo.

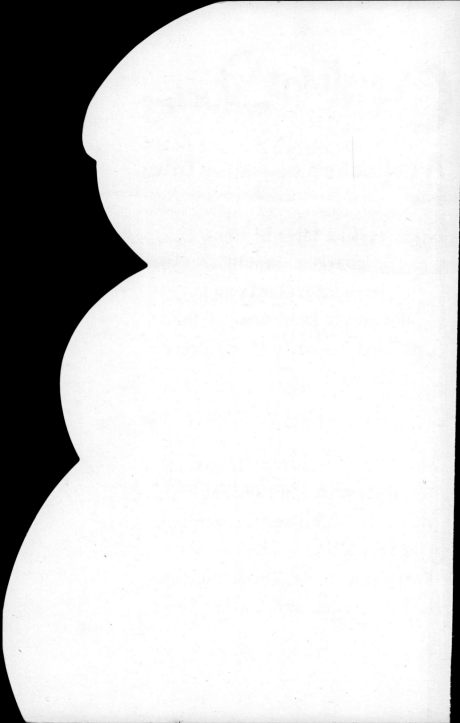